History will say little about
this monster. It will confine itself
to these words: At this time, the
internal debasement of France was
such that a bloodthirsty charlatan,
without talent and without courage,
called Robespierre, made all the
citizens tremble under his tyranny.

Pierre Louis Roederer
French Historian, 1794

D0982302

FEB 27 2009

This book is for Lisa and Joe.

Photographs © 2008: age fotostock/Classic Vision: 99; akg-Images, London/Bibliothèque National, Paris: 57, 90 top; Art Resource, NY: 88 center (Erich Lessing/Musée de la Ville de Paris, Musée Carnavalet, Paris, France), 27, 89 top left (Erich Lessing/Portraitgalerie, Schloss Ambras, Innsbruck, Austria), 10 (Erich Lessing/Private Collection); Bridgeman Art Library International Ltd., London/New York: 93 center (Bibliotheque Nationale, Paris, France/Archives Charmet), 61, 90 bottom left (Bibliothèque Nationale, Paris, France/Giraudon), 74 (Bibliothèque Nationale, Paris, France/Lauros/Giraudon), 89 top right (Chateau de Versailles, France/Lauros/Giraudon), 76 (Harris Museum and Art Gallery, Preston, Lancashire, UK), 91 top, 93 bottom (Musée de la Revolution Francaise, Vizille, France), 111 (Musée de la Ville de Paris, Musée Carnavalet, Paris, France/Archives Charmet), 91 bottom, 92 bottom right, 104 (Musée de la Ville de Paris, Musée Carnavalet, Paris, France/Giraudon), 52, 93 top (Musée de la Ville de Paris, Musée Carnavalet, France/Lauros/Giraudon), 88 top (Musée des Beaux-Arts, Lille, France/Lauros/Giraudon), 29, 80 (Ken Welsh/Private Collection); Corbis Images: 38, 89 bottom (Archivo Iconografico, S.A.), 45, 73 (Bettmann), 43 (Stefano Bianchetti); Getty Images/Hulton Archive: 68, 90 bottom right, 108; The Art Archive/Picture Desk: 88 bottom, 92 top (Marc Charmet), 113 (Gianni Dagli Orti/Musée Lambinet Versailles), 31 (Gianni Dagli Orti/Private Collection), 118; The Granger Collection, New York: 21, 91 center, 103 (Rue des Archives), 92 bottom left; The Image Works: 35, 62 (Mary Evans Picture Library), 86 (Edwin Wallace/Mary Evans Picture Library).

Illustrations by XNR Productions, Inc.: 4, 5, 8, 9
Cover art, page 8 inset by Mark Summers
Chapter art by Raphael Montoliu

Library of Congress Cataloging-in-Publication Data

DiConsiglio, John.
Robespierre : master of the guillotine / John DiConsiglio.
p. cm. — (A wicked history)
Includes bibliographical references and index.
ISBN 13: 978-0-531-18554-4 (lib. bdg.) 978-0-531-20503-7 (pbk.)
ISBN 10: 0-531-18554-0 (lib. bdg.) 0-531-20503-7 (pbk.)
1. Robespierre, Maximilien, 1758-1794—Juvenile literature. 2. Revolutionaries—France—Biography—Juvenile literature. 3. France—History—Revolution, 1789-1799—Juvenile literature. 4. France—History—Reign of Terror, 1793-1794—Juvenile literature. I. Title.
DC146.R6D54 2008
944.04092—dc22
[B]
2007037473

Tod Olson, Series Editor
Marie O'Neill, Art Director
Allicette Torres, Cover Design
SimonSays Design!, Book Design and Production

© 2008 Scholastic Inc.

Robespierre

Master of the Guillotine

JOHN DICONSIGLIO

Franklin Watts
An Imprint of Scholastic Inc.
New York   Toronto   London   Auckland   Sydney
Mexico City   New Delhi   Hong Kong
Danbury, Connecticut

The World of Maximilien Robespierre

The French Revolution was centered in the city of Paris.
But it spread throughout the entire country.

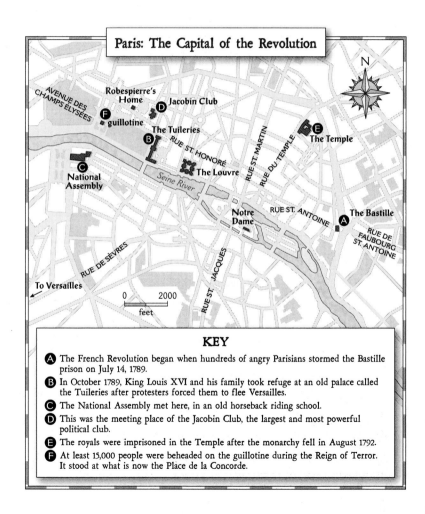

Paris: The Capital of the Revolution

Robespierre's Home — Jacobin Club — guillotine — The Tuileries — The Louvre — The Temple — National Assembly — Seine River — Notre Dame — The Bastille

AVENUE DES CHAMPS ÉLYSÉES — RUE ST. HONORÉ — RUE ST. MARTIN — RUE DU TEMPLE — RUE ST. ANTOINE — RUE DE FAUBOURG ST. ANTOINE — RUE DE SÈVRES — RUE ST. JACQUES

To Versailles

0   2000
feet

KEY

Ⓐ The French Revolution began when hundreds of angry Parisians stormed the Bastille prison on July 14, 1789.

Ⓑ In October 1789, King Louis XVI and his family took refuge at an old palace called the Tuileries after protesters forced them to flee Versailles.

Ⓒ The National Assembly met here, in an old horseback riding school.

Ⓓ This was the meeting place of the Jacobin Club, the largest and most powerful political club.

Ⓔ The royals were imprisoned in the Temple after the monarchy fell in August 1792.

Ⓕ At least 15,000 people were beheaded on the guillotine during the Reign of Terror. It stood at what is now the Place de la Concorde.

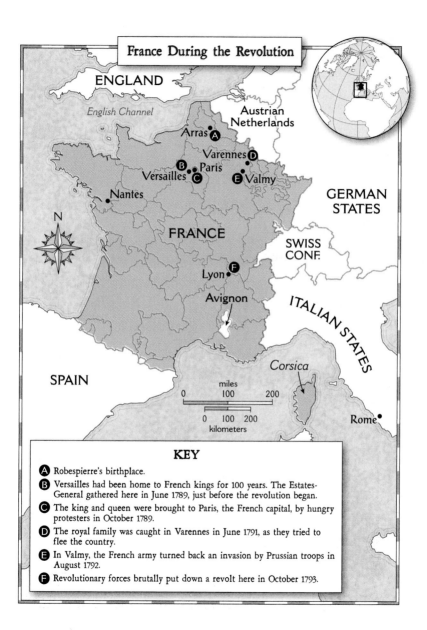

France During the Revolution

ENGLAND

English Channel

Austrian Netherlands

Arras **A**

Varennes **D**

B Paris

Versailles **C** **E** Valmy

Nantes

GERMAN STATES

N

FRANCE

SWISS CONF.

Lyon **F**

Avignon

ITALIAN STATES

Corsica

SPAIN

miles
0   100   200

0   100   200
kilometers

Rome

KEY

A Robespierre's birthplace.

B Versailles had been home to French kings for 100 years. The Estates-General gathered here in June 1789, just before the revolution began.

C The king and queen were brought to Paris, the French capital, by hungry protesters in October 1789.

D The royal family was caught in Varennes in June 1791, as they tried to flee the country.

E In Valmy, the French army turned back an invasion by Prussian troops in August 1792.

F Revolutionary forces brutally put down a revolt here in October 1793.

TABLE OF CONTENTS

The World of Maximilien Robespierre 4

A Wicked Web 8

Introduction 10

PART 1: A TALE OF TWO COUNTRIES

CHAPTER 1: Small-Town Boy 16

CHAPTER 2: A Country Divided 19

CHAPTER 3: Growing Up 24

CHAPTER 4: Power to the People 28

CHAPTER 5: Blood in the Streets 32

CHAPTER 6: Let the Revolution Begin 37

PART 2: OFF WITH HIS HEAD!

CHAPTER 7: Citizen Robespierre 48

CHAPTER 8: No Bread, No King! 54

CHAPTER 9: Man of the People 59

CHAPTER 10: Flight from Paris 64

CHAPTER 11: The Monarchy Falls 70

CHAPTER 12: The September Massacres 77

CHAPTER 13: The King Is Dead 82

ROBESPIERRE IN PICTURES 88

PART 3: REIGN OF TERROR

CHAPTER 14: The Terror Begins 96

CHAPTER 15: The Queen's Last Days 101

CHAPTER 16: End of a Friend 105

CHAPTER 17: A Final Bloodbath 109

CHAPTER 18: Live By the Mob; Die By the Mob 115

Wicked? 120

Timeline of Terror 122

Glossary 123

Find Out More 125

Index 126

Author's Note and Bibliography 128

A Wicked Web

A look at the allies and enemies of Maximilien Robespierre.

Family and Friends

FRANÇOIS ——————— JACQUELINE CARRAULT
DE ROBESPIERRE   DE ROBESPIERRE
his father   his mother

CHARLOTTE, HENRIETTE,
AND AUGUSTIN
his sisters and brother

The Royal Family and Their Supporters

LOUIS XVI ——————— MARIE ANTOINETTE
King of France; executed   Queen of France; executed
on January 21, 1793   on October 16, 1793

MAXIMILIEN
ROBESPIERRE

JACQUES NECKER   ROYALISTS   SWISS GUARD
the king's top minister   soldiers and others who   soldiers paid to
                                    sided with the king   protect the king

The Revolutionaries

GIRONDINS
moderate revolutionary leaders
who opposed Robespierre
and the Paris mob

JACOBINS
Robespierre's radical faction,
which eventually supported
the execution of the king

GEORGES DANTON
a member of the Jacobins

Assemblies and Organizations

ESTATES-GENERAL
gathering of deputies from First,
Second, and Third Estates that
met before the revolution

NATIONAL ASSEMBLY
lawmaking group formed by the
Third Estate during the early
days of the revolution

LEGISLATIVE ASSEMBLY
formed by the National
Assembly in 1791 to become the
lawmaking body of France

NATIONAL CONVENTION
elected group formed in 1792 to
write a new constitution

REVOLUTIONARY TRIBUNAL
court of 12 people formed in
1793 to prosecute and punish
people for treason

COMMITTEE OF PUBLIC SAFETY
group of nine revolutionary
leaders formed in 1793 with
dictatorial powers

MAXIMILIEN ROBESPIERRE (1758–1794)

On A SUMMER MORNING, thousands of people lined the streets of Paris to see Maximilien Robespierre taken to his death. A wooden cart carried the broken man through the crowd toward a high platform. On the platform stood the killing machine that Robespierre had made famous in recent months: the guillotine. Now it was about to be used on Robespierre himself.

Robespierre must have been a bizarre sight. He wore a fancy sky-blue coat and silk stockings. It was a formal style of dress that was already outdated. But the coat was smeared with blood. And his face was wrapped in dirty, bloodstained bandages. The night before, during his arrest, Robespierre had been shot in the jaw. It may have been a failed suicide attempt. The bullet left him almost unrecognizable.

Still, the crowd on the streets knew exactly who he was. On all sides, people shouted at him.

They threw rocks and food at his head. One woman jumped up to the cart railing and yelled, "Monster, spewed from hell!"

Robespierre showed no emotion as the crowd fought for a view of his execution. The bandage covered most of face. Only his eyes were visible to the crowd. What was he thinking behind the blank stare?

Only five years earlier, Robespierre had arrived in Paris as a young lawyer. France was on the edge of revolution, and Robespierre wanted to change the world. He believed in freedom for all people. He insisted that the poor should have the same rights as the rich.

Robespierre quickly rose to become the most powerful man in France. He helped to overthrow a king and create a new government. In the process, he won the respect of ordinary people throughout France. They hailed him as a hero of the common man.

Then the killing began. Robespierre imagined enemies around every corner. And he set out with a vengeance to protect his revolution. He sentenced thousands of people to die on the guillotine. And for a time, the people cheered every death.

Now, on that summer morning in 1794, the crowd was calling for Robespierre's own head. As his cart arrived at the platform, he could see the guillotine towering overhead. Its heavy blade hung suspended in a tall wooden frame.

No one knows what Robespierre was thinking as the executioner laid his neck under the blade. But many in Paris that day might have been wondering how a man could fall so far so quickly. How could someone who believed so strongly in the rights of all citizens have killed so many innocent people? How did France's most beloved hero turn into a monster?

PART 1

A Tale of Two Countries

CHAPTER 1

Small-Town Boy

Robespierre's parents were an
UNLIKELY MATCH.

MAXIMILIEN ROBESPIERRE'S STORY begins
100 miles from the streets of Paris. He was born in
the farmland of northern France, in a small town
called Arras. The date was May 6, 1758.

Arras was known at the time as the "city of
a hundred steeples." Everywhere visitors looked, they
saw church towers, cathedrals, and convents. The
people of Arras considered themselves religious. And
they tended to view the Parisian city folk
as sinners.

Robespierre's father, François de Robespierre, made a comfortable living in Arras as a country lawyer. His family wasn't rich, but they were well respected within the small town.

Robespierre's mother came from a different class. Jacqueline Carrault's family was poorer and less respected. They brewed beer for a living. The Robespierres probably looked down on them. They would never have picked Jacqueline as a good wife for their son.

But shortly after Robespierre's father earned his law degree, he met Jacqueline at a tavern. Not long after they met, Jacqueline became pregnant.

The news that Jacqueline was having a baby probably created a scandal. She and François weren't married. Their neighbors would have been shocked—not to mention their families. François, after all, had even studied to be a priest.

The Robespierres insisted that the couple get married. Jacqueline wasn't their idea of a suitable daughter-in-law. But the shame of an illegitimate child would have been even worse for the family's reputation.

Jacqueline was five months pregnant when she and François married. Many of the groom's family refused to attend the ceremony. The Robespierres never accepted Jacqueline. They always considered a girl from a poor family to be an unworthy wife. It was an insult that their first-born child would never forget.

CHAPTER 2

A Country Divided

Inequality made France
RIPE FOR REVOLUTION.

THE TREATMENT Robespierre's mother received from her in-laws was not unusual. At the time, France was rigidly divided by class. People born into upper-class families had rights and privileges. People born into lower-class families did not. Over a lifetime, it was almost impossible to improve one's standing.

The classes were called "estates." There were three of them, and every French person knew exactly which one their neighbors belonged to.

The First Estate was the clergy, the people who worked within the French Catholic Church. The church had enormous power and wealth. Small-town priests often lived in poverty. But the ruling "upper clergy" made fortunes by collecting money from worshippers. The priests even charged to pray for the poor in church. And the clergy paid no taxes.

The Second Estate was the nobility—people born into upper-class families. The nobility held the highest positions in the church, the army, and the government. They owned most of the land in France. But, like the clergy, they paid no taxes. They collected high rents from the farmers—known as peasants—who lived and worked on their property.

The clergy and nobility together accounted for about 500,000 of the 25 million people living in France. That's two percent of the entire population. Everyone else made up the Third Estate, the bottom rung of the class ladder. Members of the Third Estate made their living in many different ways. Some were

THE THREE CLASSES, or estates, of French society. Nobles (far left) and church leaders (middle) made up the first two estates. The other 98% of the population belonged to the lowly Third Estate (far right).

professionals who worked as doctors or lawyers, like Robespierre's father. Others worked as craftspeople, merchants, farmers, or laborers.

Some members of the Third Estate had money; others lived in poverty. But whether rich or poor, they had few rights. The Third Estate paid all the taxes. But they couldn't hold important jobs in the government or the military. If they were accused of a crime they had little chance of a fair trial.

Members of the Third Estate were often arrested for minor offenses. Nobles could get secret arrest warrants for nearly anyone who annoyed them. Police hauled people away for failing to pay their debts or getting drunk in public. Victims of the warrants could spend years in jail without ever being charged with a crime.

And for a member of the Third Estate, French prisons were a dangerous place. In prisons like the Bastille in Paris, torture was common. Food was scarce and medical care poor. The Bastille itself became famous among members of the Third Estate. No one could escape its 80-foot-high walls. People were said to disappear inside and never be heard from again.

At the top of this class system stood one person, the king of France. Like the other countries of Europe at the time, France was a monarchy—a nation ruled by a king or emperor who held absolute power. The king of France lived in luxury in a vast palace called Versailles. Located just outside Paris, the palace complex was practically a city in itself. Nearly 37,000 acres of land had been cleared for terraces and gardens. By 1775, Versailles could house up to 5,000 people. The courtyard alone held 1,400 fountains and 400 sculptures.

Outside the walls of Versailles, the people of France struggled. The poorest members of the Third Estate, peasants and laborers, lived in terrible conditions. They were heavily taxed to pay for everything from foreign wars to the king's wild parties. Food prices were so high that many couldn't afford to eat. Starvation became the leading cause of death.

At the time of Robespierre's birth, inequality in France was growing worse. The king raised taxes to pay for a war with Austria in 1740. The Third Estate also paid heavily for the Seven Years' War, which involved most of Europe from 1756 to 1763. How much longer would it take before people were ready to fight for a change?

Growing Up

Robespierre finds his way to a
good education and a brief
encounter WITH THE KING.

IN ARRAS, FRANÇOIS DE ROBESPIERRE
gained respect as a lawyer. But he had a reputation
as a hothead. He often started arguments—even
fistfights—with his friends.

François doesn't seem to have paid much
attention when his first child, Maximilien, was born
in 1758. François and Jacqueline had more children:
Charlotte in 1760, Henriette in 1761, and Augustin
in 1763.

Jacqueline raised the children with little help from her husband. But tragedy stuck in July 1764. She died giving birth. The child died a few days later. Jacqueline was just 29. Young Maximilien was only six.

Jacqueline's death threw Robespierre's father into a deep depression. He drank, borrowed money, and stayed out all night. He stopped practicing law. Sometimes he disappeared for weeks at a time. Then he reappeared to borrow more money. Finally, in 1772, he vanished for good. No one knows what happened to him. The children never saw their father again.

The Robespierre children were raised by grandparents and aunts. Maximilien was crushed by his mother's death. When he spoke about her, tears often came to his eyes. According to his sister Charlotte, the loss completely changed him. "Previously he had been like all boys, scatterbrained, wild and carefree," Charlotte wrote. "But when he realized that he was . . . head of the family, . . . he became sober, serious, and hardworking."

As a child, Robespierre had few friends. He always seemed to be in bad health. He suffered from nosebleeds that soaked his pillow in blood at night. He was small and weak, an easy target for bullies.

But Robespierre was an excellent student. He won a scholarship to the Lycée Louis-le-Grand in Paris, France's most respected university. He was just 11, which was young for a college student even in the 1700s. But, as Charlotte noted, he was a very serious boy. "There was nothing young about him," she wrote.

At Le-Grand, Robespierre was chosen for a special honor. In 1775, the school was abuzz with news. A new king had just been crowned. The young king, Louis XVI, and his glamorous wife, Marie Antoinette, made plans to visit the college. Out of 500 students, Robespierre was chosen to give a speech welcoming the royal couple.

Robespierre worked hard on the speech. He stayed up for days worrying about it. Finally, on a June afternoon, a nervous Robespierre stood outside

LOUIS XVI BECAME KING OF FRANCE when he was only 19 years old. He lived in luxury with his young wife, Marie Antoinette, in the vast palace at Versailles.

the school gates waiting for the king. It was pouring rain. Robespierre had borrowed new clothes for the occasion. They were soaked by the time the king's carriage arrived.

The king was just a few years older than the 17-year-old Robespierre. Yet Louis treated Robespierre like a child. He and his wife stayed inside the carriage. After the speech, they pulled away without giving the eager young student a greeting.

The next time the royal couple heard Robespierre's name, they would find it impossible to ignore.

Power to the People

AS A YOUNG LAWYER, Robespierre defends the little guy.

ROBESPIERRE RETURNED TO ARRAS from college in 1781. He was 5'2"—not particularly small for the time. But he seemed even tinier with his slouched shoulders and pale skin. He wore thick green-tinted glasses that he kept pushed up on his forehead. He was both nearsighted and farsighted. Throughout his life, his vision was a blur.

He was also a poor speaker. It was a time when great orators shouted in government halls. Yet Robespierre's voice was weak. His speeches were overly long.

For a time it seemed he was headed for a quiet life as a country lawyer. But Robespierre had a purpose in his life. He began to use his law practice to defend people who normally couldn't afford justice. "My life's task will be to aid those who suffer,"

AS A YOUNG LAWYER, Robespierre worked hard to protect the rights of the poor.

he told his sister Charlotte, "and to pursue . . . those who . . . enjoy the suffering of others."

In 1786, Robespierre defended a widow whose husband had been a careless spender and died in debt. According to local law, she had to pay her husband's debts—or go to prison. Robespierre argued that a widow shouldn't be responsible for her husband's carelessness. It was a radical idea for the time. But the law was abolished.

Robespierre may have had problems with another legal custom as well—the death penalty. For a time, he served as a judge. On at least one occasion, he had to sentence a murderer to death. The prisoner was to be executed by hanging, and the thought of it apparently upset Robespierre. His sister Charlotte says he didn't eat for days. He muttered, "I know he is to blame. He is a rascal . . . but to kill a man . . ."

If Charlotte's story is true, Robespierre changed his views on the death penalty drastically over the next ten years. Eventually, he would develop a strong stomach for executions.

REVOLUTIONARY IDEAS

ACCORDING TO SOME STORIES, Robespierre slept with a copy of a work by philosopher Jean-Jacques Rousseau under his pillow.

Rousseau published his famous *The Social Contract* in 1762. In it, he presented his startling ideas. Rousseau argued that the government had a responsibility to care for the people. This was radical. Most people thought the purpose of government was to make strong laws to keep people under control.

JEAN-JACQUES ROUSSEAU
(1712–1778)

According to Rousseau, government is a contract between the people and their leaders. If the leaders don't govern in a fair way, they've broken the contract. And the people would then have the right to overthrow the government.

Robespierre would later put many of Rousseau's ideas into practice—in some very radical ways.

Blood in the Streets

With the country CLOSE TO
COLLAPSE, Robespierre
seizes an opportunity.

WHILE ROBESPIERRE RAN his law practice in Arras, France was falling apart around him. The country was deep in debt. France had helped the Americans during their revolution. To pay for it, the government had once again raised taxes on the people who could least afford it: members of the Third Estate.

Before long, France went bankrupt—and the poor began to starve. The winters of 1788 and 1789 were so harsh that they became known as the Little

Ice Age. Heavy snowfalls blocked roads. Rivers froze over. When warm weather finally thawed the snow, farmlands were flooded. It was impossible to harvest grain to make bread. Bread prices soared to their highest point in 20 years. The average peasant could barely afford to feed himself and his family.

King Louis XVI wasn't blind to the chaos around him. He agreed to call a meeting of a government body called the Estates-General. French kings invited the Estates-General to meet from time to time to approve new policies or solve important problems. It included members from each of the three estates. Maybe putting all their heads together could solve France's problems.

There was one problem: No one could agree how members of the Estates-General should be chosen or how the group should make its decisions.

The Estates-General hadn't met for more than 175 years. At its last meeting, each estate met separately and voted separately. The decisions of each group were counted as one—and only one—vote. So the rich—the clergy and nobility—always outvoted the lower classes, two to one.

Now, in 1789, the Third Estate demanded power. They wanted the right to elect twice the number of representatives than they had before. They also insisted that the members of all the estates vote together. That way, the Third Estate would have a good chance at outvoting the other two estates.

In Arras, Robespierre eagerly joined the debate. He wrote pamphlets insisting that the poor deserved to have a voice in government. He viciously attacked local leaders. They refused to spend money on education and relief for the hungry, he charged. They sent people to prison without cause. Robespierre titled one of his pamphlets "Enemies of the Country Unmasked."

In April 1789, Robespierre's efforts paid off. He was elected to represent the region in the Estates-General. It was a huge step for the small-town lawyer.

AFTER HEARING RUMORS THAT THEIR WAGES WOULD
BE LOWERED, workers from a wallpaper factory attacked their boss's
home in Paris. When French troops arrived with cannons and tried to
stop the riot, it turned into a bloody battle.

As Robespierre got ready to leave for Versailles, events outside Arras made it clear that he had hard work ahead of him. Bread riots had broken out the month before in the provinces of Brittany and Flanders. Laborers joined peasants in storming bakeries. They hijacked grain wagons in the streets. The riots were often led by women desperate to feed their children.

In April 1789, the riots spread to Paris. A rumor started that a factory owner named Reveillon was planning to lower wages. At least 5,000 angry workers gathered outside his home. Waving clubs in the air, they threatened Reveillon and his family. Then they stormed the house. French troops quickly arrived, and the riot turned into a battle. By the time it was over, according to one witness, nearly 800 people lay dead in the street.

On May 1, Robespierre left Arras and headed into the chaos. As he said at the time, "Everything in France is going to change now."

CHAPTER 6

Let the Revolution Begin

The members of the Estates-General come to Versailles—and EVENTS TAKE A STRANGE TURN.

ROBESPIERRE ARRIVED IN VERSAILLES like a fish out of water. The city was the unofficial capital of the country. With 50,000 residents, it was one-tenth the size of Paris. But it was still much grander than Robespierre's hometown of Arras.

French kings had been living at the luxurious palace in Versailles for 100 years. It had become one

VERSAILLES WAS BUILT BY THE SUN KING, Louis XVI's
great-great-great grandfather. In 1789, Louis called for the
Estates-General to meet here to figure out how to end
terrible food shortages and pull France out of bankruptcy.

of the most spectacular compounds in the world. Many rooms had diamond-studded chandeliers, priceless paintings, and decorations from around the world. Most amazing was the Hall of Mirrors. Inside the room hung 17 sparkling mirrors. Each one faced a window, reflecting Versailles's vast gardens.

As Robespierre took his seat with the Third Estate, few people had ever heard of him. He was a small man with a weak voice. Not many people noticed his early speeches.

Almost instantly, the Estates-General found itself in the middle of a crisis. Members of the Third Estate demanded that all three estates meet and vote together. The clergy and the nobility refused. So, the Third Estate simply announced that they would meet to begin making decisions. Anyone who wished to join them was welcome.

On June 12, 1789, the Third Estate gathered. Only 19 clergymen and no nobles joined them. Within a week, the group had laid down a shocking challenge to the king. They gave themselves the power to make new laws for the nation. The king would have no say in their decisions. And they dared to call themselves the National Assembly.

In the royal palace, King Louis hesitated. The queen urged him to call in the army. The king's top minister, Jacques Necker, advised that he negotiate. Louis decided he would meet with all the Estates to announce a compromise. He ordered the meeting hall closed—supposedly to prepare for the meeting. The members of the Third Estate, however, did not get the message. They arrived at the meeting hall on June 20, and they were shocked to find it locked. The doors were guarded by armed soldiers.

The delegates feared the worst. Was the king trying to crush them? Were their lives in danger for questioning his authority? Would they soon be locked in the Bastille's towers?

The members of the Third Estate moved to a nearby indoor tennis court. They were determined not to back down. Together they made a pledge: They would hold firm until a constitution was written that gave equal rights to all French people. The vow was signed by 577 estate members. It soon became known as the Tennis Court Oath.

Now it was done. The Third Estate had openly defied the king. And their gamble paid off. Nobles and clergymen began to join the new National Assembly. Hungry crowds, encouraged by the revolt against the king, rioted in the streets of Paris. King Louis sent royal troops to stop the riot. But the soldiers were beginning to lose confidence in their king. Two companies of troops refused to report for duty. The next day, 48 more nobles decided to join the National Assembly. More clergy followed. King Louis was losing control of France.

A week after the Third Estate met at the tennis court, Louis officially approved the National Assembly. But that did nothing to quiet the crowds in Paris. Angry mobs attacked tollgates around the city. They burned guardhouses and broke down walls. They raided a monastery to steal grain. The king called in thousands of troops, but they couldn't stop the violence.

The city was in chaos. Troops roamed the streets. People rioted for bread. A rumor circulated that the king was planning an attack on the mob. They wanted to be ready to fight back.

On July 14, a large angry mob marched to the Bastille, the infamous Paris prison. The rioters were searching for gunpowder. But the Bastille guards were prepared. They had placed 12 big guns along the fortress's rock walls. Swiss soldiers had been hired to help fight off an attack.

But the crowd that reached the Bastille was larger—and angrier—than anyone had predicted. Hundreds of people attacked the fortress. The Swiss soldiers fought hard. But earlier that day, 300 fearful guards had abandoned their posts. Outnumbering the guards, the mob was able to push through the outer defenses.

THE FRENCH REVOLUTION BEGAN ON JULY 14, 1789,
when a mob stormed the Bastille in search of gunpowder.

At the last bridge into the Bastille, the mob
confronted the prison's governor, the Marquis de
Launay. They demanded that he lower the bridges. De
Launay refused. He claimed that he had 20,000 pounds
of gunpowder. He was willing to blow up the Bastille—
and everyone in it.

The crowd refused to back down, and De Launay finally gave in. The bridges were lowered. De Launay and his soldiers were captured. Carrying torches, the mob dragged De Launay into the streets. They stabbed and shot him again and again. Then they cut off his head and stuck it on a metal pole. The head was paraded through the streets of Paris for 24 hours before being tossed into the Seine River.

Back in Versailles, King Louis XVI learned that the Bastille had fallen. He reportedly asked an adviser, "Is this a revolt?"

The adviser responded, "No, Sire, it is a revolution."

A ROYAL MESS

LOUIS XVI WAS ONLY 19 WHEN HE BECAME KING. His wife, Marie Antoinette, was 18.

At first, the French people were fascinated by their young rulers. At Versailles, the king hunted foxes shipped to him from England. The queen held costume parties and gambling festivals.

LOUIS, MARIE, AND FAMILY

Eventually, the French started to fear that the couple did not understand the country's problems. In the 1780s, the Third Estate suffered through bread shortages and bitterly cold winters. Rumor had it that Marie's insensitive response was, "Let them eat cake."

As the king and queen grew older, they became devoted parents and decent rulers. Louis did not ignore the anger of his people. He even supported an attempt to tax the nobility.

Louis and Marie were finally ready to govern. But by that time, France was ready for them to go.

PART 2

Off
With His
Head!

C H A P T E R 7

Citizen Robespierre

The young lawyer from Arras begins to STAND OUT FROM THE CROWD.

AFTER THE FALL OF THE BASTILLE, the spirit of revolution gripped France. At Versailles, Robespierre and the National Assembly met each day. Delegates from all the estates attended. Their job was to create a constitution for France. Their meetings became a favorite event for the people of Versailles and Paris. People bought tickets to attend the debates. Every day 3,000 people packed the meeting hall.

One after another, delegates got up and argued over how France should be structured. What power should the king have? Should the church be forced to give up its wealth? Would the people have the freedom to worship as they pleased? Would newspapers be allowed to publish without censorship?

The debates stretched on week after week. Speeches often lasted for hours. One witness observed, "There were silly disputes about words . . . and dreadfully tedious posing."

Robespierre gave his share of boring speeches. But he also began to make a name for himself as one of the more radical delegates. Robespierre wanted more far-reaching changes than most of his colleagues. He demanded religious freedom and freedom of the press. He urged the Assembly not to forget the poor.

Robespierre first attracted attention a month after he arrived in Versailles. An important religious leader had come to visit the Assembly. The clergyman begged the delegates to re-think their plans for revolution. He reminded them that the poor were starving while the Assembly was stalled.

The speech enraged Robespierre. How dare a rich man lecture the delegates about the welfare of the poor! Robespierre jumped to his feet and shouted at the man. "Sell your coaches, give up your horses," he challenged. If the clergy cared so much about the poor, they should stop living in luxury. They should "convert all their . . . wealth into food for the poor," he insisted.

A hush fell over the Assembly. Several delegates whispered, "Who is that man?"

While the delegates debated, the poor continued to demand food. Ten miles away in Paris, mobs looted bakeries and other stores. In the countryside, peasants raided the homes of their landlords.

In Paris, local leaders tried to control the mob. These leaders supported the National Assembly's attack on the king's power. But they were afraid of the hungry laborers who were rioting in the streets. They formed an 800-man militia to keep the peace. It became known as the National Guard.

A general known as the Marquis de Lafayette took over command of the Guard. Lafayette had fought alongside General George Washington during the American Revolution. He had helped persuade Louis XVI to send soldiers to America. Lafayette supported the revolution in France. He hoped a new French government would give the people many of the same rights the Americans had fought for. But he was still loyal to the king.

By August 1789, the crowds in the streets were getting out of control. The National Assembly decided to act. In one 24-hour session, the delegates passed a mountain of laws giving rights to the poor. The church could no longer demand money from its worshippers. Landlords would no longer hold power over the peasants who worked their land. Nobles and common people would pay the same taxes.

A MAN SHAKES OFF HIS CHAINS and reaches for a gun, while a nobleman and a clergyman look on in terror. This illustration is called *The Awakening of the Third Estate, July 1789.*

Criminals would be punished equally, whether they were rich or poor.

In a single day, the National Assembly had wiped out the old French legal system. And they didn't stop there. They created their own bill of rights, called the Declaration of the Rights of Man and of the Citizen.

This document was passed on August 26, 1789. It condemned governments that favored the rich over the poor. It insisted that a country's leaders must be responsible to its citizens. And it promised a new government that would protect everyone's right to liberty, equality, and full citizenship.

In another part of Versailles, Louis had a decision to make. The Assembly had not mentioned the king in its declaration. It had not demanded that Louis step down. But it had made it clear that monarchy had no place in the new France. Would Louis support the Assembly's decisions or reject them? The king decided to do nothing.

The next step in the revolution was left to the people in the streets.

No Bread, No King!

WITH PARIS STARVING, Louis is
thrown out—and Robespierre wins
friends among the people.

IN OCTOBER 1789, PARIS WAS HIT with two
different kinds of floods. One was a constant, hard-
falling rain. It soaked the streets for weeks. The other
was a flood of angry, hungry peasants.

Unemployment was running high. Bread prices still
had not dropped. Workers gathered often to protest in
the streets. The atmosphere was tense.

Near the end of September, two events pushed the
mob into violence. First, a regiment of royal troops

arrived in the city. Rumors spread fast. Was the king planning a counterrevolution? By now the National Guard numbered 30,000. But could it stand up to the king's army?

Then, on October 1, news leaked out about a party at Versailles. Toasts were drunk to the royal family. The king and queen were applauded. When they left, they supposedly trampled the three-colored ribbon, an important symbol of the revolution.

The news was just enough to send the crowd over the edge. On October 4, hungry and desperate Parisians murdered a baker. A large crowd gathered. Lafayette and his National Guard struggled to keep order.

The next day, a mob of 7,000 marched from Paris to Versailles in a heavy rain. Most of the protesters were women. They arrived in Paris soaking wet and covered in mud. They demanded to see the National Assembly.

Robespierre met with 12 of the group's leaders. He heard their pleas for food. And he promised to investigate the cause of the food shortages. He may even have hinted that the king wanted his people to starve.

The women left the Assembly believing that Robespierre was their ally.

That night, leaders of the protest sent word to the king. They wanted him to leave the plush rooms and gardens of Versailles. He belonged in Paris, they said, where the people could keep an eye on him.

The king told his guards to prepare for the worst. They blocked the doors to the palace. Still, the protesters managed to force their way inside. A crowd of wet and muddy women swarmed the palace. They ran through the kitchen and ate any scraps of food they could find. The king's bodyguards tried to stop them. Fighting raged on through the night.

Trapped in his rooms, King Louis decided there was no point in fighting. He ordered his bodyguards not to resist. He agreed to accept the Declaration of the Rights of Man. And he offered to send sacks of

PROTESTERS FORCED LOUIS AND HIS FAMILY from the palace
at Versailles. As the king retreated to Paris, he watched the mob parade
the heads of his bodyguards through the streets.

flour to Paris to feed thousands of hungry people.

Then, surrounded by the crowd, Louis, Marie, and their supporters left for Paris. People yelled at them along the way. Outside his carriage, the king saw the severed heads of his bodyguards on pikes.

In Paris, Louis and Marie took refuge in a dusty old palace called the Tuileries. In the coming months, crowds often gathered outside to protest. Marie Antoinette complained that when she opened a window for fresh air, people threw rocks and garbage at her.

The mob had driven the king and queen from their home. The power of the common people was growing in France. And Robespierre was quickly becoming their spokesman.

CHAPTER 9

Man of the People

ROBESPIERRE SPEAKS OUT
and makes a friend for life.

ROBESPIERRE FOLLOWED THE KING AND QUEEN to Paris. Versailles, after all, was the symbol of the old monarchy and its injustices. Paris would be the home of the new government.

There, the king was nearly a prisoner in his own palace. He was forced to accept his new role. He would be ruled by the laws of the constitution.

The National Assembly met in an old horseback riding school near the Tuileries. The space was small compared to Versailles. Only 200 spectators could crowd into it. Parisians who wanted to watch the revolution in progress had trouble finding tickets.

The delegates split into groups, or factions. And they spent most of 1790 arguing over the constitution.

One of the most powerful factions was called the Jacobins. It was headed by Robespierre. He and the rest of the party sat in the highest chairs. They looked down on the rest of the delegates. Because of their lofty position—and their growing power—they became known as the Mountain.

With Robespierre leading the way, the Jacobins pushed the Assembly into more radical moves. The Assembly's first target was the clergy. "Church property belongs to the people," Robespierre argued. Most of the delegates agreed. In November, they seized all church property for the government. Their plan was to sell the land and use the money to pay for the revolution.

The Jacobins also declared that religious leaders should be elected by the people, instead of appointed by the Pope in Rome. And they insisted that all bishops and priests swear an oath of loyalty to the new French government. Those who did could continue their work. Those who refused could be accused of treason.

THE JACOBINS BECAME A POWERFUL FORCE during the revolution. Jacobin clubs like this one in Paris sprang up all over France in the the early 1790s.

In these debates, Robespierre won a reputation as a completely devoted revolutionary. He didn't drink or gamble. He didn't make much money and never took bribes. He lived simply in the back room of a carpenter's house. Although women adored and even babied him, he probably never had a serious romance. Before long, people called him the "Incorruptible."

In the Assembly, Robespierre made an unlikely friend. His name was Georges Danton. Like Robespierre, he was devoted to the revolution. And like Robespierre, he sided with the common people.

But although they agreed on politics, Danton and Robespierre had little else in common. Robespierre was slight and frail. Danton, on the other hand, was a

GEORGES DANTON BECAME
Robespierre's closest political ally, and
possibly his closest friend.

bear of a man. He was barrel-chested with a booming voice. He had a huge appetite for wine and women. And while Robespierre rarely admitted that he might be wrong, Danton was more willing to forgive his enemies.

Still, the two became close friends. When Danton's wife died, Robespierre wrote to comfort his grief-stricken friend. "I love you until death," he told Danton.

But as the revolution went on, Robespierre would grow more and more suspicious. He began to treat even his closest friends like enemies.

CHAPTER 10

Flight from Paris

As war threatens, the king and his family try to escape THE REVOLUTION.

ROBESPIERRE SAW ENEMIES of the revolution everywhere. And in part, he was right. The king still had supporters all over France. Wealthy landowners hated the new laws passed at the beginning of the revolution. They wanted their old privileges restored. Many priests refused to swear loyalty to the new government. They preached against the revolution in churches around the country. Some army officers were still loyal to the king as well.

Outside France, the royal courts of Europe watched the revolution with fear. The countries surrounding France were all monarchies. They were shocked by the sight of a king becoming a prisoner in his own country. What would happen if the unrest in France spread beyond its borders?

Since the beginning of the revolution, French nobles had been escaping to Austria and to Prussia (Germany). These exiles urged the leaders of both countries to invade France and return Louis to power.

The emperor of Austria, Leopold II, also had a personal connection to the French royal family. He was Marie Antointette's brother. According to rumors, he was planning to rescue his sister and brother-in-law and crush the revolution. Some even said that Austrian troops had gathered along the French border.

In Paris, the Assembly debated how to handle the foreign threats. Some argued that France should go to war to save the revolution. Others called for peace. Neither Robespierre nor Danton wanted to fight. They both thought that war could destroy all the gains they had made so far.

In February 1791, the streets of Paris erupted in violence once again. Inside the Tuileries Palace, the royal family feared for their safety. Marie wanted the family to flee before the mob turned on them. Louis resisted at first. But his wife and his advisers pleaded with him. If the royal family were safe, they might still be able to save the monarchy.

The king agreed to a plan. A group of soldiers loyal to the king was camped near the border with the Austrian Netherlands, 170 miles away. The king would try to reach them and set up a base on the border. Austrian soldiers would assure their safety.

On June 20, the royal family and their closest servants fled Paris in secret. They disguised themselves as the friends and family of a Russian baroness. They sneaked into carriages in the middle of the night.

Suddenly, Marie gasped. Lafayette's own carriage had galloped past. For an instant, a light from the carriage swept over Marie's face. She ducked inside, worried that they had been caught. Inside the carriage, their sleepy daughter asked her older brother where they were going. "To act in a play, I suppose," he said, unsure why they were dressed so strangely.

The Royal Flight, as it was later called, made it as far as the small town of Varennes. There, a merchant recognized Louis from his face on a coin. Two days later, the family was brought back to Paris. The National Guard led them through the streets of the capital. Crowds of people watched the royal family return in disgrace.

Robespierre was furious—and terrified. He told his friends that the king's flight was surely part of a plot against the revolution. Assassins were probably waiting to kill the leaders of the Assembly. Robespierre was certain he would be one of the first to go.

In the meantime, there was business to attend to. Robespierre spoke at a Jacobin gathering in Paris.

PEASANTS ARMED WITH FARM TOOLS hold Louis and his family captive. The royals had been caught in the town of Varennes, while trying to escape to the Austrian Netherlands.

The king, he said, had shown himself an enemy of the revolution. His escape attempt proved that the revolution was in danger.

Then Robespierre stared into the crowd. He insisted that the enemies of the revolution were everywhere. They sat in the Assembly. They could be sitting next to anyone in the room. "Look around you," Robespierre told the Jacobins. "Share my fear."

Here was a sign of things to come. Robespierre had begun to imagine enemies all around him—even among his friends. Perhaps it was something in his voice that night, but no one stood to challenge him.

Robespierre ended by insisting that he was ready to give up his life for the revolution. Someone in the room stood and shouted, "We would all give our lives to save yours!"

CHAPTER 11

The Monarchy Falls

France gets a new constitution—
AND THEN GOES TO WAR.

IN THE SUMMER OF 1791, most of the Assembly did not share Robespierre's fear—or his ideas about the king. Robespierre wanted the king arrested and put on trial for his escape. The National Assembly, however, forgave Louis. The delegates simply weren't ready to get rid of the monarchy altogether.

The Assembly returned to its business. In September 1791, the long-awaited constitution was finished. It did not go as far as Robespierre had wanted. But it did take away most of the king's power.

There would now be a permanent legislature in France called the Legislative Assembly. Its job would be to make laws. Like a president, the king would put the laws into practice. He could also veto, or cancel, laws for five years. But he could not interfere with the legislature's work in any other way. In fact, he couldn't even call himself a king. Louis was given the title "First Functionary of the State."

All of Paris celebrated the constitution. Robespierre and his allies were led through the city by an admiring crowd.

The small-town lawyer had come a long way in the previous two years. No one had heard of him when he arrived in Paris. Now, he was a hero among the people of France. When he visited his hometown of Arras, crowds cheered him. "Vive Robespierre!" they shouted. "Long live the defender of the people!"

But several months later, the revolution was in danger. By early 1792, Austria and Prussia had agreed to attack France.

In response, France declared war on Austria on April 20, 1792. Fighting began at the border. And soon, Lafayette and his army began to lose ground.

Then, in July, word reached Paris that Prussia had joined the war against France.

The Legislative Assembly decided to act. They ordered fresh soldiers to come to protect Paris. The order was a direct attack on the king's power. Even under the new constitution, Louis was supposed to be in charge of military operations. But the Assembly was convinced that the king did not want France to win the war.

The king threatened to veto the order. Despite his threat, the troops began to arrive. The Prussian commander, from his post at the border, issued a warning to the people of France. He wanted to protect the royal family, he said. If Louis and his family were hurt, he would march on Paris and destroy the city.

To the people of Paris, the Prussian's warning was proof that the king was a traitor. Louis seemed

A FRENCH SOLDIER ASSISTS A WOUNDED COMRADE during the war against Prussia and Austria. The ruling families of Europe were terrified that revolution would spread from France.

to be plotting with his royal allies in Austria and Prussia.

On August 10, a crowd formed near the Tuileries. It grew to 20,000 angry rioters. The king's advisers

THE MONARCHY FINALLY FELL when an angry mob of 20,000 stormed the Tuileries Palace on August 10, 1792.

begged Louis to flee. At first, the queen said they should stay and fight. The Tuileries was well armed with guards from Switzerland and other troops loyal to the king. But an adviser told Marie the truth: "Madame," he said, "all of Paris is against you."

The king and queen fled to the Legislative Assembly next door. Soon after, the mob stormed the old palace. The National Guard joined the protesters. The Swiss soldiers opened fire on them all. Hundreds of protesters were killed. But others eventually reached the Swiss and hacked them to pieces. When the massacre was over, the rioters burned the bodies of the Swiss soldiers in celebration.

The king and queen of France no longer had a palace of any kind. In the Assembly meeting hall, they were taken to a side room. National Guard troops kept watch over them. Inside the main room, the Assembly officially took away the king's power. The king and queen were now just ordinary citizens—and prisoners at that. Guards escorted the family to a prison tower in Paris.

For Robespierre, the storming of the Tuileries was an even greater day than the fall of the Bastille. The people, he said, had taken matters into their own hands. He praised them for protecting

"justice, equality, and reason against their enemies."
The monarchy had fallen at last. The revolution,
Robespierre thought, was back on track.

AFTER AUGUST 1792, LOUIS AND MARIE ANTOINETTE were
just ordinary citizens, with no royal privileges. The entire family was
imprisoned in the Temple, an ancient fortress in Paris.

C H A P T E R   1 2

The September Massacres

Panic and hunger lead to BRUTAL RIOTS in Paris.

WHOEVER CONTROLLED THE MOB controlled France. That was a lesson Robespierre had learned quickly. But in the fall of 1792, all of France discovered another truth.

Sometimes the mob couldn't be controlled.

The fall of the king did little to improve the lives of most people in France. Prussian troops invaded France on August 19, 1792 and moved toward Paris.

Poverty and hunger were still widespread all across the country.

In Paris, groups of working people met to plan protests. Often the violence erupted without any planning at all.

The mobs of angry citizens became known as the *sans-culottes*. In French the name indicated that they didn't wear the short pants that upper-class men wore. They dressed in the more humble clothes of shop owners, craftsmen, or day laborers.

After the storming of the Tuileries, the *sans-culottes* held great power over the revolution. Their leaders governed Paris in a group called the Commune. They pushed the wealthier leaders of the revolution for more radical changes. They wanted a limit set on the price of bread and other food. They wanted a National Convention to write a new constitution. Its members would be elected by the people. And all male citizens would be allowed to vote.

The Legislative Assembly stalled on the economic demands. But they agreed to disband in favor of a National Convention.

Robespierre applauded the decision. He didn't always agree with the *sans-culottes*. But he realized that the future of the revolution rested in their hands. His speeches to the Jacobins began to sound like he approved of the violence in the streets. "We must exterminate those miserable villains who are [plotting] against the rights of man," Robespierre insisted. "We must exterminate all our enemies."

Encouraged by the fall of the king, the mob acted out Robespierre's commands. For a week, the streets of Paris exploded in violence. The riots became known as the September Massacres.

The clergy were the first victims. On September 2, guards were taking 24 priests to prison for refusing to take the oath of loyalty to France. A mob attacked the group. The priests tried to lock themselves in the prison. But the mob dragged them into the streets and

ROBESPIERRE TOLD THE POOR to "exterminate those miserable villains" who opposed the revolution. In September 1792, a mob attacked this monastery and killed more than 100 priests.

murdered them. The next day, a monastery was attacked. More than 100 priests were killed with long stakes.

Next, the mob attacked Marie Antoinette's closest friend, the Princess de Lamballe. The princess was being held in a prison. But the mob broke down the walls. The *sans-culottes* ordered the princess to swear her hatred of the king and queen. When she refused, she was stabbed with a sharp stake. According to some stories, the mob ripped the princess's heart from her body. Her head was cut off and placed on a stake. The crowd then marched to the fortress where the king and queen were held. When the queen came to the window, the mob tossed her friend's head at her balcony.

In less than a week, the *sans-culottes* killed more than a thousand people. Most of the victims weren't nobles. Many were common people, imprisoned for debt or prostitution. The massacre was gruesome. In the months to come, Robespierre's friend Danton heard the victims screaming in his nightmares.

Robespierre never spoke a word about the massacres. He never showed any signs of guilt. As he put it: "Pity is treason."

CHAPTER 13

The King Is Dead

At Robespierre's urging, France EXECUTES its former ruler.

AFTER THE SEPTEMBER MASSACRES, Paris settled down for a time. The Prussian invasion stalled when French troops won an important battle at the town of Valmy.

In late September 1792, delegates to the new National Convention met for the first time. Their purpose was to write a new constitution. This time, it appeared, the constitution would not include a king.

Robespierre was once again at the center of the debate. He had gotten himself elected to the new

Convention. His first act was to get their meeting place moved. He wanted a hall big enough for crowds. With "the people" watching, Robespierre felt, the Jacobins would be able to dominate the Convention.

For two months, the delegates argued. The Convention was split into two main factions: the Girondins and the Jacobins. The Girondins were more cautious than the Jacobins. They spoke out strongly against the September massacres. And they opposed the demands of the *sans-culottes*.

When the Convention met, the Girondins attacked Robespierre immediately. He held too much power over the mob in Paris, they claimed. Robespierre and Danton fought back. "Who dares accuse me?" Robespierre shouted at the delegates. He went on to accuse his enemies of treason.

In the meantime, Robespierre wasn't taking any chances. He was convinced that assassins were plotting to kill him. He had a bodyguard with him at all times.

In November, the Convention turned to its most pressing issue: What should they do with the king? Many delegates thought it was too dangerous to keep him as a prisoner. As long as he stayed in prison, his allies would be tempted to free him. Other delegates insisted that the king had committed treason by plotting against the revolution—and that he should be put on trial.

Robespierre proposed a different solution. No trial was necessary, he said. Every step of the way, he said, the king had opposed the revolution. Only under pressure did he accept the new laws of the assemblies. He plotted with his foreign allies to destroy the revolution. It was clear that Louis was an enemy of the people. For his crimes, he should be executed. "The king must die so that the country may live!" he insisted.

What happened to Robespierre's famous hatred of the death penalty? Robespierre had an explanation for his change of heart. Before the revolution, the death penalty had been used by the rich and powerful against "the people." Now, he argued, it should be used by the people against their enemies. The king had committed treason by opposing the revolution. Therefore, he deserved to die.

In December, the delegates ordered the king to appear before the Convention. For several days, Louis answered questions about his actions during the revolution. Then he was sent back to prison. The Convention voted and the debate was over. The king was guilty of treason.

On January 21, 1793, Louis XVI awoke to the sound of drums outside his jail cell. The night before, he had said goodbye to his wife and children. The couple that started as mismatched teens had grown to love each other. Louis promised Marie that he would see her again in the morning. But it was a lie. He couldn't stand to say goodbye.

A crowd gathered to watch the king's death. He tried to say a few words. But his speech was drowned out by the drumbeats. He asked the guard

ROBESPIERRE AND HIS ALLIES sentenced King Louis XVI
to death by guillotine. The king said to the jeering crowd:
"I die innocent. . . . I pardon those who have occasioned my death."

not to tie his hands. His request was refused. Louis put his neck below the blade. The king of France was beheaded quickly. The executioner held his head up for the cheering crowd to see. The mob ran to the guillotine and plunged their hands into Louis's blood. In a wild dance, they sprinkled each other with the king's blood.

Marie Antoinette heard the frenzied cries from her prison cell. Moments later, a jailer appeared at her door. He handed her Louis' wedding ring. The queen collapsed in grief when she realized her husband was dead.

That morning, Robespierre ate a peaceful breakfast in his room. The king passed by Robespierre's door on his way to the guillotine. But the Incorruptible had boarded the windows. There was no need to see the king's last moments.

Robespierre in Pictures

YOUNG IDEALIST

As a young man, Maximilien Robespierre worked as a lawyer in his hometown in France, defending the poor.

CRUSHED

In Robespierre's day, the poor paid heavily to fund the church and the army. This political cartoon shows a farmer crushed by this burden.

TENNIS COURT OATH

In 1789, Louis XVI called for a meeting to discuss France's problems. Before the meeting started, delegates from the working class met at this tennis court and demanded a greater role in the country's politics.

LET THEM EAT CAKE

Louis and his wife, Marie Antoinette, lived extravagantly in Versailles. They eventually became responsible leaders. But by then, the public hated them.

STORMING THE BASTILLE

The French Revolution began on July 14, 1789, when a mob stormed a prison called the Bastille to free its prisoners and seize ammunition.

MOB RULE

On October 5, 1789, protesters marched to Versailles to demand food. They attacked the palace and, as shown here, killed some of the king's bodyguards and put the heads on stakes. The royal family fled to Paris.

THE INCORRUPTIBLE

Robespierre got the nickname "The Incorruptible" for his commitment to the revolution.

ROBESPIERRE'S RADICALS

Robespierre's faction in the National Assembly, the Jacobins, pushed for the most radical changes. Their supporters formed Jacobin clubs, like this one in Paris.

ROYAL FLIGHT

The royal family tried to flee France in June 1791 but was caught in the town of Varennes.

TAKING IT TO THE STREETS

Crowds of working men called *sans-culottes* demanded more rights and cheaper food. Robespierre tried to ally himself with them.

THE KING MUST DIE

Robespierre called loudly for the king's execution. Here, Louis says a final goodbye to his family in January 1793.

SPREADING TERROR

The Revolutionary Tribunal was formed in October 1793 to convict and execute suspected traitors.

INSTRUMENT OF TERROR

"We must exterminate our enemies," said Robespierre. During the Terror, (September 1793 to July 1794), at least 15,000 were beheaded by the guillotine.

LAST OF THE GIRONDINS

The Girondins, once leaders of the revolution, were condemned as traitors by Robespierre. Many were led to the guillotine.

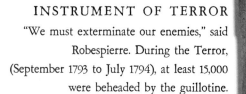

QUEEN CONVICTED

Marie was forced to plead her case before the Tribunal. She was sentenced to death and sent to the guillotine in 1793.

THE TIDE TURNS

People began to wonder if Robespierre was going too far. In this editorial cartoon, he has put everyone in hot water— and rescued only a few.

ROBESPIERRE'S TURN

As his former friend Danton had predicted, Robespierre's own head soon came under the guillotine.

PART 3

Reign of Terror

The Terror Begins

Robespierre gets new power—
AND USES IT.

IN 1793, FRANCE SLID TOWARD CHAOS. The new government was fighting enemies from all sides.

By early that year, France's neighbors—Austria, Prussia, Spain, the Netherlands, and Great Britain— had agreed to oppose the revolution. For them, the execution of Louis XVI had been the last straw. The prime minister of Great Britain called it "the foulest . . . deed [in] the history of the world."

Already at war with Austria and Prussia, France now declared war against Great Britain.

And inside France, there were enemies everywhere. French troops struggled to crush royalist revolts across the country.

In Paris, the king's death failed to quiet the *sans-culottes*. In March, they took to the streets again. Robespierre had begun criticizing the moderate Girondins as wealthy enemies of the revolution. The mob responded by destroying Girondin newspapers. They burned offices and smashed printing presses.

At the same time, Robespierre and other members of the National Convention worried that they were losing control of the revolution. Danton proposed an idea. He suggested creating a Revolutionary Tribunal. Its 12 members would form a kind of court. Their job would be to judge suspected enemies of the revolution. They would have the power to arrest people for treason. And they would quickly impose punishment. The punishment for treason, of course, was death.

The Tribunal would extend throughout France. Towns across the country would form watch committees to keep an eye on all foreigners and suspected traitors.

Robespierre supported Danton's plan. They both hoped that the Tribunal would bring peace to France. It would crush the royalist rebels and quiet the mob by reassuring them that enemies of the revolution were being punished.

The Convention also created a new group with enormous powers. It was called the Committee of Public Safety. Its nine members would work in secret to direct the Tribunal and the army.

The mob, however, was not appeased. At the end of May, crowds of angry Parisians forced their way into the Convention. They wanted a limit on food prices. They wanted the rich taxed to feed the poor. The Girondins, they insisted, were blocking their proposals. They demanded that the Girondins be thrown out of the Convention.

Robespierre saw a chance to get rid of his political enemies. He sided with the *sans-culottes*. And on June 2, 1793, with a crowd of 80,000 surrounding the

STILL STARVING, THE *SANS-CULOTTES* DEMANDED
more executions. Robespierre was happy to oblige. Here, his political
enemies, the moderate Girondins, are led away to prison.

Convention, it was done. Nearly 30 Girondins were
sent to jail to await their trials for treason.

In September, violence flared up again. A rumor
spread through Paris that royalists planned to invade
the city. Hungry and scared, the Parisian mob rioted.
They called for more executions. And Robespierre
responded.

Robespierre had been elected to the Committee
of Public Safety. He and his allies declared terror

"the order of the day." Then they gave the Tribunal terrifying power by passing the Law of Suspects. The new law allowed the Tribunal to execute all people who "showed themselves . . . to be enemies of liberty." People who wrote or spoke a word against the revolution could be found guilty. So could those who associated with known "enemies of the people."

The Tribunal acted quickly. During the last three months of the year, 177 Parisians died at the guillotine. Outside Paris, the violence was equally shocking. In Lyon, revolutionaries brutally put down a royalist rebellion. Nearly 2,000 prisoners were tied in a line and shot by cannons. In Nantes, men, women and children were tied naked to old boats. Holes were punched into the hulls and the boats were launched. The victims begged for their lives as they sunk to the bottom of the river.

The Terror had begun. And Robespierre welcomed it. "We must exterminate all of our enemies," he said, "with the law in our hands."

CHAPTER 15

The Queen's Last Days

Marie Antoinette falls victim to THE GUILLOTINE.

Soon, THE TERROR REACHED THE FORMER QUEEN. Since the storming of the Tuileries, Marie and her children had been kept together in a prison in Paris. But after Louis's death, Marie's son, eight-year-old Louis-Joseph, was taken from her. Guards had to pry the boy from Marie's arms. Later, a fence was built around the prison gardens where Marie exercised. Robespierre wanted to make sure she couldn't see her child. Eventually, the queen pulled a slice of wood off the fence to peek at her little boy. He was dressed in the long pants of a *sans-culotte*. Someone had given him a toy guillotine to play with.

In October 1793, Marie was dragged before the Tribunal. Its members spent two days accusing her of crimes against the nation. She responded with quiet dignity. "I was a queen, and you dethroned me," she said. "I was a wife, and you murdered my husband. I was a mother, and you have torn my children from me. I have nothing left but my blood. Make haste to take it!"

Robespierre worried that the crowd would start to support Marie. But the Tribunal wasted no time. The former queen of France was sent to the guillotine at noon on October 16. Her husband had been allowed to travel to his death in a closed carriage. She was taken in an open cart. Crowds shouted at her as she passed. Like her husband, she passed Robespierre's apartment on her way to the guillotine. Once again, he barely noticed.

Marie climbed the steps to the guillotine. She was just 37, but she was thin and gray. She looked nothing like the lively young queen who had been both loved and hated by France. As she stood next to the guillotine, she accidentally stepped on the executioner's foot. "Monsieur, I ask your pardon," she said. "I did not do it on purpose." Those were her last words.

ONCE A BEAUTIFUL YOUNG PRINCESS, Marie died a broken woman. The revolution had taken her husband, her children, and now her life.

THE GUILLOTINE

IT WAS THE INSTRUMENT OF TERROR DURING THE FRENCH REVOLUTION. But it was considered a humane way to execute people.

For centuries, the French government had executed criminals by hanging, shooting, or burning them. Many were tortured first. Often, the victims suffered intensely before they died.

Only the nobility were beheaded. But even this form of execution was sloppy. It often took several blows.

A Jacobin named Dr. Joseph Guillotin proposed another way to separate heads from bodies.

"YOU'LL NEVER FEEL IT," Dr. Guillotin said of the guillotine.

The device was a heavy blade hung in a tall wooden frame. The blade was raised with a rope—and then dropped on a victim's neck. As Dr. Guillotin put it, "With my machine, I'll knock your head off in the twinkling of an eye, and you'll never feel it."

End of a Friend

As heads roll, old friends become NEW ENEMIES.

ROBESPIERRE WAS NOW at the height of his power. And the executions continued. The victims were not limited to nobles and clergy. People accused of hoarding food went on trial. Farmers who refused to give up their grain to the urban poor were accused of treason. Robespierre's political enemies also found their way to the guillotine. On October 31, 1793, 21 of the Girondins arrested in June had their heads cut off.

In Paris, the executions became a popular pastime. Large crowds gathered around the guillotine. They elbowed their way to the best views. Parents brought their children to cheer when the executioner raised a severed head. Vendors even sold programs listing the names of the doomed prisoners.

As the killings went on, Danton grew sickened by them. He had proposed the Revolutionary Tribunal to keep the peace. But there were now fewer threats to the revolution. And still, the guillotine continued to claim more and more victims.

In March 1794, Danton took Robespierre to dinner. The bigger man clapped Robespierre's frail shoulder and begged him to end the Terror. The executions had to stop. "Royalists and conspirators I can understand," Danton said. "But what about those who are innocent?"

Coldly, Robespierre replied: "And who says anyone innocent has perished?"

Danton must have realized that his friend was beyond reason. Robespierre argued that everyone must do what is best for the people. Danton challenged him: Who was to decide what was best for the people? Without hesitation, Robespierre replied that *he* would. After all, he was the Incorruptible.

Danton may have seen how blind his old friend had become. The goal of the revolution had been to fight injustice in France. Now it was killing innocent people. And Robespierre did not see the problem.

Danton may also have known that after arguing with Robespierre, he did not have long to live. Some say that as Robespierre left the table in anger, Danton's eyes filled with tears.

Later that night, Robespierre told the Tribunal to arrest Danton. The Tribunal charged Danton with conspiring to overthrow the government. Danton responded by listing all the things he had done for the revolution. He ended by saying, "I would embrace my worst enemy for the sake of the country, and I will give her my body if she needs the sacrifice."

The Tribunal found Danton guilty. On April 5, 1794, he went to the guillotine. Standing at the killing machine he spoke his final words: "This time 12 months ago, I proposed this infamous Tribunal by which we die and for which I beg pardon."

BEFORE DANTON WAS EXECUTED, he predicted that "Robespierre will follow me" to the guillotine.

CHAPTER 17

A Final Bloodbath

Robespierre tries to remake France—
WITH THE GUILLOTINE
AS HIS TOOL.

DANTON'S DEATH seemed to have little effect on Robespierre. He showed no regret. If anything, Danton's trial convinced Robespierre that his suspicions were correct. The revolution was in danger from all sides. The police needed to work even harder to punish the enemies of the people.

Robespierre pushed for even tighter laws. He wanted all foreigners and nobles kicked out of Paris. And he insisted on tighter control of trials. From now on, political prisoners from all over France were to come to Paris to be judged.

Robespierre had a plan for France. Good citizens in the new France, he insisted, must think of the country first and themselves last. They must devote themselves completely to the revolution.

Robespierre wanted nothing less than to remake the entire country. Already the work had begun. In October, the National Convention had created a new calendar. History, they claimed, should begin with the fall of the monarchy. September 22, 1792 had been the day the Convention officially abolished the monarchy. So that day became the beginning of Year I. All months were renamed. Sundays and popular Christian festivals were erased from the calendar.

Robespierre even tried to create a new religion. Everyone should worship a "Supreme Being," he said. Every ten days, people would celebrate a holy day. Each day would have a different focus. The French people would spend their holy days worshipping "liberty and equality," "the martyrs of freedom," and "hatred of tyrants and traitors."

The first of these festivals fell on June 8, 1794. All of Paris was decorated with ribbons and flowers. Nearly everyone in the city came out for the celebration. Thousands of people gathered at the Tuileries to hear Robespierre speak. He wore a sky-blue jacket and a

ROBESPIERRE WANTED TO CREATE a new religion for France. To celebrate the first new holy day, he organized an elaborate "Festival of the Supreme Being" in Paris.

large sash. Robespierre and the Convention deputies led the crowd on a parade through the city. Along the way he could hear some of his colleagues laughing at his elaborate rituals. But he was convinced, as always, that the people were with him.

Two days after the festival, Robespierre got another terrifying law passed. From now on, the Revolutionary Tribunal could impose only one sentence on the suspects it found guilty. It had to sentence them to death. At the same time, the list of crimes got longer. It included lying to "the people," stealing public property, and producing spoiled food.

Robespierre now devoted himself to a single task. He tried to manage the huge number of treason cases generated by the revolution's spies. People all across France sent reports exposing "enemies of the people." Robespierre spent hours reading the reports and deciding who should be arrested.

Over the next six weeks, many hundreds of people were snatched up by police. Most of them were innocent of any crime. Many were accused by neighbors who wanted their land or property. Some were turned in by personal enemies.

The Tribunal became a factory, churning out guilty verdicts. Robespierre ordered it to "conclude

DURING THE TERROR, Robespierre and his allies packed the prisons with people they suspected of treason.

every case within 24 hours." Victims were dragged into the courtroom in the morning. By noon, they had their sentence. By 3:00 P.M., their hair was shaved and their hands were tied. They were sent in carts to their deaths.

The guillotine worked overtime. Between June 10 and July 27, 1794, 1,366 people were executed. On the worst days, three dozen people could be sent to the guillotine. The device eventually had to be moved outside the center of Paris. The blood was polluting the city's drinking water.

The killings were shocking. Yet Robespierre was convinced they were necessary. He had a vision of a new France, a peaceful, democratic country that would be a model for the rest of the world. In his view, whatever it took to make that vision a reality was justified. "Terror is only justice," Robespierre said. "Prompt, severe, and inflexible."

Live By the Mob; Die By the Mob

As the Terror runs its course, time runs out for the INCORRUPTIBLE.

FINALLY, THE MOB IN THE STREETS began to grow tired of the Terror. Each day more people died under the guillotine. But conditions weren't improving. There was still no bread. People still lived in poverty. And France was making progress in its European wars. The idea that the Terror kept the nation secure from foreign threats seemed absurd.

Robespierre may have realized that he was losing his hold over the *sans-culottes*. He was also losing his power in the Committee of Public Safety. Some wanted to end the Terror. Others simply felt Robespierre was getting too powerful. And the supporters of Danton wanted to avenge their leader's murder.

As usual, Robespierre went on the attack. On July 26, 1794, he appeared before the Convention. His words were familiar by now. There were conspiracies everywhere. "Spies are hired and stationed in our public places," he claimed. Always, Robespierre said, he was the victim of lies.

Then Robespierre told the Convention that it was time to arrest a new group of plotters—men who were sitting in the room. Yet he refused to reveal their names. The members of the Convention shifted in their seats. No one knew who might be the next to go before the Tribunal.

Finally, though, Robespierre had misjudged his colleagues. The Convention spent two hours debating their response to the speech. An angry deputy got up and dared to insult Robespierre. "It is time to tell the whole truth," he announced. "One man is paralyzing the National Convention. That man is Robespierre."

The next day, Robespierre returned. When he rose to speak, the deputies began to shout. "Down with the tyrant!" they screamed. "Down with the tyrant!"

When the deputies settled down, they voted for Robespierre's arrest.

Robespierre still had plenty of supporters in Paris. The city's jailors refused to hold him prisoner. Robespierre and several allies hid in an old hotel and plotted their next move.

But late that night, soldiers broke into the hotel. They had correctly guessed the password—"Vive Robespierre!" They burst into Robespierre's room. Shots were fired. One of Robespierre's friends held two pistols. He handed one to Robespierre—and used the other to shoot himself. In the confusion, Robespierre was shot in the jaw. No one knows whether a soldier shot him or he tried to kill himself.

The bullet tore off much of the Incorruptible's face. Lying on a stretcher, bleeding badly, he was carried to the Tuileries. He wasn't expected to live through the night. But when a doctor arrived in the morning, Robespierre was awake. He was ready for his trip to the guillotine.

Like the thousands of people he sent to their death, Robespierre was paraded through the streets

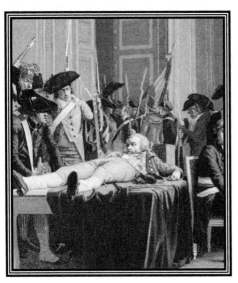

WHEN THE FRENCH CITIZENS grew tired of Robespierre's Reign of Terror, the National Convention voted to arrest him. Here, Robespierre lies badly injured, surrounded by his captors.

in an open cart. He wore the same sky-blue jacket he'd worn at the Supreme Being festival. Now it was covered in blood.

By now, the mob had turned on their hero. They shouted and threw rocks and garbage at him. A woman jumped to the railing of the cart. "Go now, evil one," she shouted in his face. "Go down into your grave with the curses of the wives and mothers of France."

Robespierre walked up the steps to the guillotine. The executioner stripped off the blue jacket. Before he bent Robespierre's head to the blade, he violently ripped off the bandage holding his face together. Robespierre let out a howl of pain—just as the guillotine's blade sliced through his neck. On July 28, 1794, Robespierre was dead.

Wicked?

Robespierre was just 36 when he bowed before the guillotine. In many ways, he'd had a remarkable life. He helped end the rule of kings in France. He fought to give people equal rights under the law. Some of his ideas were way ahead of their time. He wanted to tax the wealthy and use the money to help the poor. He insisted that everyone had the right to an education.

Yet Robespierre is not remembered for these ideas. He is remembered for the execution of thousands of innocent people. In Paris today it's easy to find statues of revolutionary heroes like Danton. Only one metro station carries Robespierre's name.

It's hard to understand exactly how Robespierre fell so far. Most historians agree that he was not just hungry for power. He was a different kind of tyrant, one who is truly committed to a cause.

"He'll go far," one of Robespierre's rivals once said of him. "He believes everything he says."

Robespierre had a vision for France. He believed so firmly in his vision that he never once doubted that he was right. When people argued with him, he dismissed them out of hand. Anyone who did not agree with him was not only his own enemy— but an enemy of France.

The revolution—Robespierre's vision of it— became so important to him that he would do anything to help it succeed—even create a state of terror. To Robespierre, the ends justified the means. In other words, remaking France was so vital that killing a few thousand people did not seem like a crime. "Terror," he said, "is justice."

Timeline of Terror

1758

1758: Maximilien Robespierre is born in Arras, France.

1764: Robespierre's beloved mother, Jacqueline, dies during childbirth.

1769: Robespierre attends the Lycée Louis-le-Grand in Paris.

1775: Louis XVI is crowned king of France.

1781: Robespierre returns to Arras to practice law.

1788: Louis XVI agrees to convene the Estates-General.

April 1789: Robespierre is elected to the Estates-General.

June 1789: The Third Estate breaks from the Estates-General to form the National Assembly.

July 1789: A mob invades and destroys the Bastille prison in Paris; this starts the French Revolution.

October 1789: Women protesters force Louis and his family to move from Versailles to Paris.

1791: The royal family attempts to escape the country. They are stopped at Varennes and become prisoners.

April 1792: France declares war on Austria.

September 1792: During the September Massacres, mobs around the country kill more than a thousand people.

January 1793: King Louis XVI is executed for treason.

September 1793: The Reign of Terror begins.

July 1793: Robespierre is voted to the Committee of Public Safety.

June 1794: Robespierre is mocked at the Festival of the Supreme Being.

October 1793: Marie Antoinette is executed.

1794

GLOSSARY

abolish (uh-BOL-ish) *verb* to officially put an end to something

assassin (uh-SASS-in) *noun* a person who murders a well-known or important person

avenge (uh-VENJ) *verb* to obtain satisfaction by punishing a wrongdoer

bankrupt (BANGK-ruhpt) *adjective* unable to pay one's debts

chaos (KAY-oss) *noun* total confusion

class (KLASS) *noun* a group of people in a society with a similar way of life or range of income

clergy (KLUR-jee) *noun* people trained to conduct religious services

conspiracy (kuhn-SPIHR-us-see) *noun* a secret, illegal plan made by two or more people

constitution (kon-stuh-TOO-shuhn) *noun* the system of laws in a country that state the rights of the people and the powers of the government

delegate (DEL-uh-guht) *noun* someone who represents other people at a meeting

estates (ess-TATES) *noun* the name given to the three different classes in French society before the revolution

execution (ek-suh-KYOO-shun) *noun* the act of killing someone as punishment for a crime

exterminate (ek-STUR-muh-nate) *verb* to kill large numbers of people or animals

faction (FAK-shun) *noun* a party or group within a government that has its own goals

Girondins (je-RAHN-dins) *noun* a moderate political faction in Paris during the revolution; the Girondins became increasingly unpopular because they supported saving the king's life

guillotine (GEE-uh-teen) *noun* a large machine with a sharp blade used to sever the heads of criminals

illegitimate (il-uh-JIT-uh-met) *adjective* born to an unmarried mother

incorruptible (in-kuh-RUHPT-uh-bul) *adjective* incapable of being tempted to do bad or dishonest things

Jacobins (JAK-uh-bins) *noun* the most powerful and radical political group during the revolution; they supported voting rights and education for the poor, but used their power to eliminate their enemies

legislature (LEJ-iss-lay-chur) *noun* a group of people who have the power to make or change laws for a country or state

monarchy (MON-ark-ee) *noun* a country led by a ruler who inherits his or her position

monastery (MON-uh-ster-ee) *noun* a group of buildings where monks live and work

nobility (noh-BIL-ih-tee) *noun* the people in a country or state who have been born into wealthy families and have the highest social rank

radical (RAD-i-kuhl) *adjective* believing in extreme political change

revolution (rev-uh-LOO-shuhn) *noun* an uprising by the people of a country that changes the country's system of government

sans-culottes (SOHNZ-coo-LOT) *noun* the most radical group of peasants in France; their name means "without breeches" to distinguish them from the breech-wearing men of the nobility

treason (TREE-zuhn) *noun* the crime of betraying your country by spying for another country or helping an enemy during a war

vengeance (VEN-juhnss) *noun* punishment inflicted in retaliation for an injury or offense

veto (VEE-toh) *verb* to stop a law from being enacted

FIND OUT MORE

Here are some books and Web sites with more information about Robespierre and his times.

BOOKS

Gilbert, Adrian. **The French Revolution.** New York: Thomson Learning, 1995. (48 pages)
A fast and easy-to-read guide to the French Revolution.

Lotz, Nancy and Carlene Phillips. **Marie Antoinette and the Decline of French Monarchy (European Queens).** Greensboro, NC: Morgan Reynolds, 2005. (160 pages)
An engaging biography of Marie Antoinette.

Plain, Nancy. **Louis XVI, Marie-Antoinette, and the French Revolution (Rulers and Their Times).** New York: Benchmark Books, 2001. (88 pages)
Learn how the royal couple lived—and how they died—in this short biography.

Scandiffio, Laura. **Evil Masters: The Frightening World of Tyrants.** Toronto: Annick Press, 2005. (230 pages)
Profiles of history's worst monsters, from Ivan the Terrible, to Robespierre, to Saddam Hussein.

WEB SITES

http://chnm.gmu.edu/revolution
This comprehensive site, Liberty, Equality, Fraternity: Exploring the French Revolution, is a collaboration of the Center for History and New Media at George Mason University and the American Social History Project at City University of New York. It includes real letters and documents from the revolution, along with 245 images, maps, and even songs.

http://encarta.msn.com/encyclopedia_761557826/French_Revolution.html
MSN Encarta's online encyclopedia article on the French Revolution.

http://www.pbs.org/marieantoinette/
This companion to the PBS special Marie Antoinette and the French Revolution *includes a timeline, stories of royal life, and details about the revolution. Don't miss the "famous faces" portrait gallery for a profile of "Mad Max" Robespierre.*

For Grolier subscribers:
http://go.grolier.com/ searches: French Revolution; Robespierre; Danton; Louis XVI; Marie Antoinette; guillotine; Paris; Versailles; France

INDEX

American Revolution, 32, 51

Arras, 16, 28, 32

Austria, 23, 65, 71

Austria and Prussia, war with, 72–73, 77, 82, 96, 115

Austrian Netherlands, 66, 68

Bastille, 22, 42–44, 89

bread riots, 36, 42

Brittany, 36

calendar, new, 110

church property, seizure of, 60

clergy, 20, 61, 79-80

Committee of Public Safety, 98, 116

Commune, the, 78

constitution, 48–49, 60, 70

Danton, Georges, 62–63, 65, 97–98, 106, 108

debtors' law, abolishment of, 30

Declaration of the Rights of Man, 52–53, 56

de Lamballe, Princess, 80–81

England, war with, 96

Estates-General, 33, 39

executions, 100, 105-106, 112-114

Festival of the Supreme Being, 110–111, 119

First Estate, 20

Flanders, 36

France, economic problems of, 32–33, 38

French Revolution beginning of, 43, 44 opposition to, 64–65, 96

Girondins, 83, 92, 97, 98–99

Guillotin, Dr. Joseph, 104

guillotine, 11, 13, 92, 100, 102, 103, 104, 106, 108, 114, 115

Incorruptible, the, 62, 87, 90, 107

Jacobins, 60–61, 79, 83, 90

king, powers of under constitution, 71

Lafayette, Marquis de, 51, 72

land ownership, 20

Launey, Marquis de, 43–44

Legislative Assembly, 71, 72, 79

Leopold II, emperor of Austria, 65

Little Ice Age, 32–33

Louis-Joseph, Prince, 101–102

Louis XVI, King ascension to throne, 27 capture in Varennes, 67, 68, 91 and Estates-General, 33, 40 execution of, 85–86, 91 "First Functionary of the State," 71 flight to Austria, 66–67, 91 imprisonment of, 75, 76 move to Tuileries Palace, 58 reign of, 45, 89 and speech by Robespierre, 26, 27

Lycée Louis-le-Grand, 26

Lyon, 96, 100

Marie Antoinette, Queen capture in Varennes, 67, 68, 91 execution of, 93, 102–103 flight to Austria, 66–67, 91 imprisonment of, 75, 76, 101 move to Tuileries Palace, 58 rumors about, 45, 55

mobs, 42, 44, 50, 55, 58, 66, 90, 98

monarchy, definition of, 22
monarchy, fall of, 74—76
monasteries, attacks on, 42, 80
Nantes, 100
National Assembly, 40-41, 48-49, 51-52, 65, 70
National Convention, 78, 79, 82—85, 97, 110, 116—117
National Guard, 51, 55, 75
Necker, Jacques, 40
nobility, 20
Paris, 22, 26, 36, 41, 42, 50, 55, 58, 59, 66, 71, 72, 78, 98—99, 111
prisons, conditions in, 22
protests by workers, 78
Prussia (Germany), 65, 71, 77, 82, 96, 115
Reign of Terror, 118
Reveillon, 36
Revolutionary Tribunal, 92, 97, 102, 112
riots, 35, 36, 41—44, 50—51, 73—75, 79, 99
Robespierre, Augustin de, 24
Robespierre, Charlotte de, 24, 25, 26, 29, 30
Robespierre, François de, 17, 24, 25
Robespierre, Henriette de, 24

Robespierre, Jacqueline Carrault de (mother of Maximilien), 17—18, 25
Robespierre, Maximilien
    arrest of, 11, 117—118
    assessment of, 120—121
    childhood, 16, 24—26
    creation of new religion by, 110—111
    death penalty, opposition to, 30
    description of, 28—29
    early ideals of, 12, 28, 49—50, 30
    education, 26
    election to Committee of Public Safety, 99
    election to Estates-General, 34
    election to National Convention, 82—83
    execution of, 12, 93, 119
    friendship with Danton, 62—63
    Incorruptible, the, 62, 87, 90, 107
    and Jacobins, 60, 79, 90
    as lawyer, 29—30, 88
    loss of power, 116—117
    mother's death, effect of, 25—26
    position on foreign threats, 65
    respect for, 12, 60, 62, 71
    speech for King Louis XVI, 26—27

    suspicious nature of, 63, 67, 69, 83, 109, 116
Rousseau, Jean-Jacques, 31
Royal Flight, the, 67
sans-culottes, 78, 79, 80—81, 83, 91, 97, 98, 116
Second Estate, 20
September Massacres, 79
Seven Years' War, 23
social classes, 19—23
Swiss Guard, 42, 74, 75
taxes, inequality of, 20, 21, 23, 32
Temple, the, 76
Tennis Court Oath, 41, 88
Terror, the, 100, 101, 113, 115
Third Estate, 20—23, 34, 39—41
Toulon, 96
Tuileries Palace, 58, 74, 111
Valmy, 82
Varennes, 67, 91
Versailles, 22—23, 37—39, 55, 57
Versailles, assault on, 56
Washington, George, 51
women, protests by, 36, 55—56, 90

Author's Note and Bibliography

History doesn't know what to make of Maximilien Robespierre. Was he a revolutionary fighting for the downtrodden? Was he a hero of the common man? Or was he a mass murderer? Was he a paranoid fanatic who made speeches about the rights of citizens—even as he sent thousands of them to their deaths?

Robespierre is a complex and confusing character. It's the historian's job to solve mysteries like these, to figure out how a man like Robespierre inspired a nation to horrible extremes. And it's not an easy task. When writers of current nonfiction do research, they rely on events they've seen with their own eyes. Or they interview witnesses. That's impossible when you're writing about someone who died more than 200 years ago.

Instead, historians turn to primary sources—actual documents from the time their subjects lived. That can mean letters or diaries, family documents or medical records. Historians also rely on research of other writers.

Several sources were invaluable to me in writing this book:

Banfield, Susan. **The Rights of Man, the Reign of Terror: The Story of the French Revolution.** New York: Lippincott Williams & Wilkins, 1990.

Furet, Francois and Denis Richet. **The French Revolution.** New York: Macmillan, 1970.

Jordan, David P. **The Revolutionary Career of Maximilian Robespierre.** Chicago: University of Chicago Press, 1989.

Kekes, John. "Why Robespierre Chose Terror." **City Journal** (London), Spring 2006.

Linton, Marisa. "Robespierre and The Terror." **History Today,** August 2006.

Schama, Simon. **Citizens: A Chronicle of the French Revolution.** New York: Alfred A. Knopf, 1989.

Scurr, Ruth. **Fatal Purity: Robespierre and the French Revolution.** New York: Henry Holt and Co., 2006.

Liberty, Equality, Fraternity: Exploring the French Revolution website. Center for History and New Media at George Mason University and the American Social History Project at the City University of New York.

—John DiConsiglio